# Melissa's Animals
# and Other People

# Melissa's Animals and Other People

pictures by Melissa E. Roy

verses by Klaus G. Roy

The Wooster Book Company
Wooster, Ohio • 2006

# The Wooster Book Company

*where minds and imaginations meet*

Appreciation is extended to the following organizations for permission
to reprint some of the drawings from their previous publications:

• The Musical Arts Association, operating The Cleveland Orchestra

• *Key Concert* programs of the Junior Committee of The Cleveland Orchestra

• The Suburban Symphony Orchestra, Beachwood, Ohio

• *Cleveland Magazine*

• David, Sharon, and Helena Richardson for their recommendation
of The Wooster Book Company

ISBN 10: 1-59098-456-0
ISBN 13: 978-1-59098-456-7

# A Greeting from the Picture Maker

Hello, and welcome to the wild and woolly (or feathered!) world of the
teresting characters who live in this book!

When I made these drawings, I was a child like you, from age six to twelve.
nly a few of the pictures are from a couple of years later—you can probably tell
ich ones. I must have liked animals a lot, and looked at them as friends.
ey most probably were!

Growing up, I always had dogs plus an assortment of gerbils, hamsters, mice,
arakeet, and I once had a kitten named Mittens. We had to give him up when he
came a cat and we found out that my Dad, my brother, and I were allergic to him.

Now I am a lot older (in my forties, believe it or not!). My Dad, who is much
der yet, naturally, is a writer and composer. More than thirty years after these
tures were drawn, he made up those verses to go with them. Maybe they will
ve you and your folks a chuckle or two!

Many years ago, my father also wrote a whole opera for performance at the
eveland Zoo, and called it *The Enchanted Garden* or ... the *Zoopera*! He must
ve liked animals too, (still does!), because everybody in the opera is one ... except
e Princess, of course.

I hope you will have as much fun with these pictures as I had drawing them so
any years ago. It seems as though I always had a felt-tipped pen and a pad of paper
my hands back in those days. Why not have those handy too, and as you are
oking at this book, start sketching your very own *Animals and Other People*.

Have a good time on your visit to my menagerie!

— *Melissa*

**A fiddle-playing Elephant —**
**Now that is really elegant!**

**A trumpet lesson from a Pachyderm —
Might it not make a nervous Monkey squirm?**

**This Puppy plays a silver flute;**
**When it grows up, what will it toot?**

**This Horse can play the harp with feeling;**
**Her tail makes music quite appealing.**

**Let's jump and dance and sing and play —**
**It's raining Cats and Dogs today!**

**We've no idea who this is;**
**If you can tell, you get a kiss.**

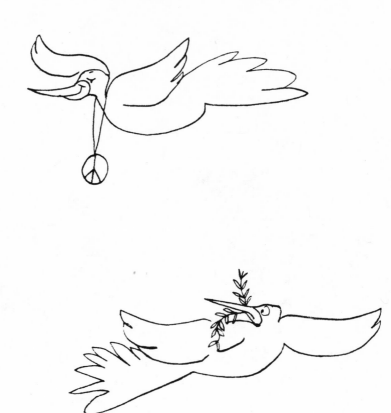

**It's fair to say you risk defeat**
**When you seek peace with such conceit.**

**Just scratch my back, and you will hear
What lovely music will appear!**

**What bird would play the double-bass?
It plucks the strings with utmost grace.**

**You'd have to be a big and patient bird
to get your beak-string plucked.
But that's absurd!**

This **Cheshire Cat** is not all there ...
But it won't fade away, I swear!

**Why can't a little dog have nightmares too?**
**When I wake up, watch how my bite scares you!**

**This Beagle,** we think, is not very cheerful;
It looks to us worried, or a little bit fearful.

Here are sights of special joy:
A lively dog with a happy boy!

This high-strung **Bull** looks rather scary:
I'd rather fight a dromedary.
Or, if you like, a cassowary!
(You'll find it in your dictionary.)

**This has to be the strongest Monkey!
Some find such heavy lifting funky.**

**Be careful when you snap that pouch —
Your Kangaroolets might cry "ouch!"**

**Don't let this pompous Dragon scare you:
He huffs and puffs—but just to dare you!**

When all the creatures get together
To sing and dance in perfect weather,
It's grand how they all get along
With cheerful dance and merry song!

**This Horse can run a good deal faster
With rollerskates—a racing master!**

This **Leopard** wants to take his spots off,
But thinks—those fleas! Will there be lots of?

**For this Bird, learning French is fun;**
**A record shows him how it's done.**

**This Cuckoo Clock** will only chime
**When it decides to tell the time.**

**This Fossil rolls inside its rock;
It needs a carbon-dating clock!**

**This Bird sings loudly and secure in pitch;**
**But it's the same each time, without a glitch!**

**Is this a Hobbyhorse, or what?**
**A fine guitar will help it trot.**

**A Mouse's** tail is good to tweak;
That makes it musically squeak!

**This very gifted Phonocat**
**Plays any tune for mouse or rat.**

This cool **Cat** plays the gramophone;
It does so with its tail alone.
If it were tall, like a giraffe,
It couldn't play the phonograph.

**Most Ants walk horizontally;
But here's one upright, frontally!**

**A Hedgehog** on his nose? That pricks!
No **Seal** should have to do such tricks.

**This special kind of Zebra does its grazing
With music that to us sounds quite amazing!**

**These animals are really sharp:**
**A cymbal-oboe, horn, and harp!**

**A baritone sax espies a lonely cello;**
**The music they could make is really mello!**

**He doesn't really need his trunk key
To toss about his friend, the monkey.**

**Why do these Fish do such a dance,**
**Behaving like comedians?**
**They know if there is lots of laughter**
**They will be thrown some crumbs thereafter.**

**This sadly unemployed Giraffe
Delivers grapefruit. Don't dare laugh!**

**These monsters we can't figure out;
Can you tell what they're all about?**

These creatures are a mystery;
Are they from ancient history?

**This Camel's** humps are rather lumpy;
That makes the desert ride quite bumpy.

**When two Wolves** are enjoying their cocktails,
That's a good time for planning some stock sales.

**Of all our many friendly creatures,**
**These two may have the oddest features.**

**The Crocodile** is not a kindly beast;
His dentist must be a percussioneest.

**To practice scales on scales is rather easy,**
**If Dinosaurs don't make you somewhat queasy.**

These wise old **Owls** both went to Yale;
This **Mouse** won't live to tell the tail.
(Watch your spelling!)

This **Lion**, jumping through his hoop,
Feels like a stupid loopy dupe.
In fact, he is so bored and sleepish
That he acts absolutely sheepish.

It's true: one **Mouse** could make one wary;
But, half-a-dozen ... Now, that's scary!

You know the story when the **Lion**
got hurt with a thorn in his paw; how fateful!
A kindly **Mouse**, brave, death-defying,
dared take it out! But was he grateful?

We know some **Dads** who smoke a pipe;
We like that warm and smelly type.

It seems to us that neither **Pup**
Cares which is down and which is up.

**This wasn't always just a game ...**
**We like to play it, just the same.**

**Can anyone become a music-maker?**
**A Hippo drum and a Soprano faker?**

**Here is a friendly Bloodhound!**
**Let's see what he has found.**

**A Pharaoh is an Egyptian king;**
**This may be one, or quite another thing.**

**This well-dressed Penguin drank too much ...
Don't drive!
Go dive and catch some fish, and stay alive.**

It's quite **OK** sometimes that you are scared;
But you'll feel better when your fears are shared.

We wonder what will happen with this dog ...
Make up your own tale for your private log.

If a couple is happily married,
They wouldn't be bothered or harried
If they had a nice dog for a pet!
Would the family then be all set?

**But these, you say, aren't animals ...
Watch out—they might be cannibals!**

# Fisher man and his cat

4/69

fairy forest

4/69

**This seems to be another cool pet dragon!
Let's take him home in our volksy wagon.**

# The Crab Story

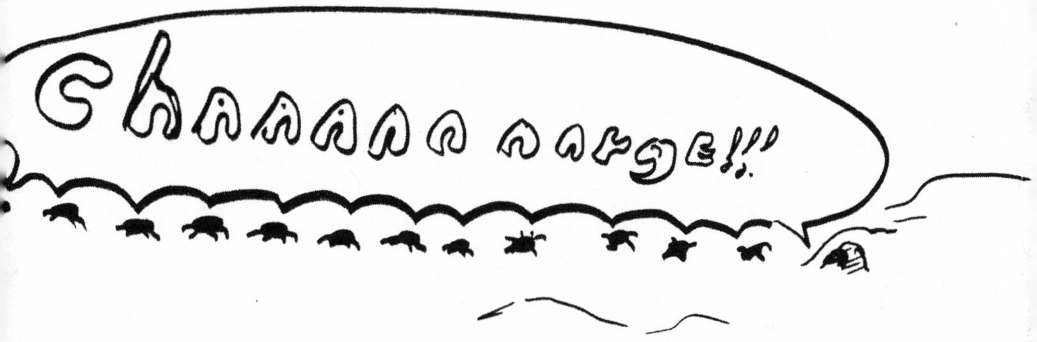
Chaaaaa aarge!!

u have surely heard a performance of Sergei Prokofiev's delightful musical story ut Peter catching the Wolf with the help of his friends the bird and the cat, d how at the end "you can hear the duck quacking inside the wolf, because in his ry he had swallowed her alive!"

Quack Quack Quack Quack

This **Wolf** is caught in **Peter**'s noose;
There's little chance he could get loose.
But even if he did—hold steady!
Brave Peter has his popgun ready.

**Although the picture's rearranged,**
**The story hasn't really changed;**
**So here is Peter once again,**
**And our Wolf still growls ... in vain!**

85

Here are four of the seven pictures drawn by Melissa Roy, at the age of eleven, during the premier performance of *Platero and I* by Juli Nunlist, given by the Suburban Symphony Orchestra at Cleveland State University on Sunday, April 23 1972, under the direction of Robert C. Weiskopf. The work is described as a tone poem based on various episodes in the life of the donkey Platero and the Spanish poet Juan Ramón Jiménez, who wrote over one hundred prose poems about their life and travels together.

This is the world's most famous Donkey,
As stubborn as a mule or monkey.
Señor Jiménez told his story;
Read it some time! You won't be sorry.

# A Draw-Bridge from the Past to the Present

Children's books are almost always written for them by adults. It is very rare for a child to produce enough usable pictures to make a book. Here is such a one, with most of the drawings dating from age nine to twelve.

Melissa Roy, born in Cleveland in 1960, began to draw, as virtually all children do, at three. By the age of seven, it had become a daily routine, with up to ten pictures a day, and it did not cease for a decade, when she was seventeen and ready for college. A BFA degree from Kent State University (1982) was the culmination of academic art work perhaps not quite as spontaneous as the thousands of drawings she had made as a child.

Her work was first published when she was ten. For five years she provided the illustrations for the young children's concerts at Severance Hall, home of the renowned Cleveland Orchestra, and when she was twelve an entire spread of her pictures appeared in an issue of *Cleveland Magazine*.

Numerous pieces were used for family Christmas cards, and two drawings done at Interlochen at age fourteen were printed on the covers of special concerts by The Cleveland Orchestra. Some thirty of the drawings made in 1970–1972 graced the pages of her father's book of essays published by the Orchestra on the occasion of its seventy-fifth anniversary in 1993.

The accompanying verses were composed by the young artist's father some thirty years after the pictures were originally made without any awareness of their possible utilization. Melissa (Mrs. Neal J. Legger of Brunswick, Ohio) is now a married lady in her mid-forties, and she looks at her childhood production as if it were virtually from someone else's hand.

What a child sees and imagines cannot be recaptured wholly by a mature adult; a few great artists like Paul Klee and Joan Miró come close to suggesting the freshness of childhood inspiration, but from a highly experienced and sophisticated standpoint. Prodigious early creativity remains a wondrous and cherishable aspect in the making of art.

"I have known Melissa Roy as a child-artist for some years. She had imagination and remarkable ability to animate. It was something I had never seen in a child's work before …"
—JOHN TEYRAL (college recommendation, 1977)
Distinguished artist-teacher of The Cleveland Institute of Art

"I'm astounded at Melissa's drawings … Such talent and humor!"
—ELEANOR WORTHEN (1973)
Western Reserve Academy, Hudson, Ohio

"Your daughter's drawings are most striking … A stimulating experience to share!"
—MORTON GOULD (1971)
Composer and Conductor, New York

"Melissa—Your drawings in *Cleveland Magazine* were absolutely charming, in addition to being amusing and edifying … Your observations of behavior and emotion between animals and people are just right!"
—DAVID S. LEVENSON (1973)
Director of Public Relations, The Cleveland Orchestra

"Melissa's drawings fairly leap off the page …"
—from letters

**Melissa E. Roy** (Mrs. Neal J. Legger of Brunswick, Ohio) was born on October 6, 1960, in Cleveland, Ohio. She is a graduate of Glen Oak School (now part of Gilmour Academy), and holds a BFA from Kent State University. She is currently working in the health care field.

Between 1968 and 1978, Melissa produced some 20,000 drawings in black on white, with her first publications at the age of ten, mostly for The Cleveland Orchestra's *Key Concert* programs for young children. When she was twelve, *Cleveland Magazine* published a two-page spread of her pictures. Drawings by her have appeared in numerous venues, some thirty of these in the collections of her father's program book essays published by The Cleveland Orchestra in 1993.

Photo: Christopher Roy

**Klaus G. Roy** was born in 1924, in Vienna, Austria. He has lived in the United States since 1940, and served in the U.S. Army from 1944 to 1946. A graduate of Boston University and Harvard (1947 and 1949), he has worked as composer, teacher, music critic, music librarian, lecturer, and author of light verse. From 1958 to 1988, he served as program annotator and editor of The Cleveland Orchestra, publishing thirty volumes of program notes. A collection of his special essays from these volumes was published by the Orchestra in 1993, under the title ***Not Responsible for Lost Articles***, in observance of the ensemble's seventy-fifth anniversary.

Photo: Eric Christian

Other children's books published by
# The Wooster Book Company

*Warm as Wool*, written by Scott Russell Sanders and
   illustrated by Helen Cogancherry
*Scamper: The Bunny Who Went to the White House*,
   written by Anna Roosevelt and illustrated by Marjorie Flack
*A Nest of Bluebirds*, written and illustrated by Rose Marie Scott
*The Gentle Ones*, written and illustrated by Rose Marie Scott